You can see John and Don now sitting on a porch every night.
They tell stories about the time the Ninja Gator gave them a fright.
Sometimes when they tell the stories, they look sad and blue.
Curious though...
in their story the brothers ate the gator at a barbecue.

If you head out to the marsh when the day loses its hue,
there's a chance you could meet the Ninja Gator, too.
He's got Ninja wisdom that he's ready to pass right along.
And, if you listen closely, the frogs now sing Ninja souds, too!

John and Don look at each other and look rather sad.
This strange Ninja spell is driving them mad!
But surrounded by armored snakes, there is nothing
else they can do.
They agree to the terms.
Their hunting days are through.

The brothers are told they can hunt no more.

If they want to eat, they have to go to the grocery store.

They can not ever chase a frog around a log again.

If they do, they will become redneck s'mores for all the

Ninja gator's friends.

But it does not stop there – no, it goes on.

You see, the brothers can not even take a gun further than

their lawn.

They have to leave all their hunting equipment at home.

If they do otherwise, they will be eaten where they roam.

"Now boys," Ninja Gator says, "I know this will be hard to

understand."

"But you can still use your guns in the yard."

"Now leave us alone and we'll leave you alone, too!"

"Just realize that your redneck hunting days are through."

The brothers get their wits back and try to fight.
Turns out the snakes have bulletproof vests, too!
The shots from Jon and Don just bounces away.
The snakes are about to win the day!

As the snakes begin to storm in,
Jon notices in the back stands an alligator with a grin.
"That dadnabit Ninja Gator has come to take our souls!" he cries.
"This isn't the day I want to die."

Then the Ninja Gator yelles out "STOP!"
It becomes so quiet that you could hear someone open a soda pop.
"Let this be a lesson," the Ninja Gator says.
"The next time you hunt in my marsh, you brothers will wind up
dead!"

The Ninja Gator has a whole list of demands.
He puts the list into each brother's hands.
"Let's go over what you can and can't do."
"Let's face it, boys. Ninja Gator don't want to eat you!"

Meanwhile the family holds a yard sale to sell some of their most valuable possessions like decoys and hunting gear and just everything they have assembled from around the country.

The twin brothers are still on the lookout for that gator that is still sneaking around in the woods and they don't exactly appreciate the fact that their wives and kids go on about this ridiculous weekend holiday sale.

The aligator is nowhere to be found and that's why the twins are gearing up for a nasty battle.

YARD
SALE

Next the brothers become the town's teacher's worst nightmare because they have another hunch about where the gator might hide.

They hear something in the radio about an aligator that is crawling around in the neighborhood.

Jon & Don want to be good neighbors and they want to save the kids at school from this event.

Later it turns out the aligator thing was just a Southern joke from the radio host.

Both rednecks do not believe the freaky joker and stay alert while playing some poker.

Jon charges in hard and straight.

Don tries to change up things with a different gait.

Both brothers quickly hit their first hackey sacks quite true,

but then something happens – and neither brother knew

what to do!

You see, snakes converge on them from everywhere.

The brothers try to run, but they can not go anywhere!

"Oh Jon!" Don cries. "I'm sorry I'm better than you!"

The next day comes as a chance of changing trouble into peace.
It is Hacky Sack day and it would be as fun as fun could be!
To win, one brother has to shoot 10 hacky sacks with a confirmed hit.
The loser would have to clean the winner's hunting kit.

Jon was excited to prove that he was the superior one.
It didn't matter if it had been three years since he'd won.
Today was the day that everything would finally change.
It was time to make become a redneck that was disarranged!

Don, for his part, was ready to make hackey sack art.
He would move faster than a Walmart shopping cart!
The two brothers shared a glare as the time counted down to one.
Then, with a quick whistle, the hackey sack wars had begun!

But the next day, Jon knows he needs to prove his brother wrong.
He goes and buys that Pom before too long.
Jon is going to show Don that small dogs are the best hunting
dogs. Poms can really crawl into logs to scare out the frogs!

So Jon meets Don that night for another hunting trip.
When Don sees the little dog, the jokes begin to rip.
"What do you call the smallest hunting dog in the word?"
Don asks Jon.
"You call it liquid in a snake's drinking flask!"

"And what kind of hunting can you do with what a small dog can
catch?"
"Why you can play an awesome game of fetch!"
And despite the high hopes that Jon has for his little pom,
that puppy is unable to catch one single frog.

"Real men hunt with real dogs," Don says to Jon.
"Hunting with rats like these is worse than having no fun!"
The Pom begins to run and hide from insulting Don.

Jon & Don, on the other hand, have no clue what just happened
and totally ignore the Samurai's mission.

"You don't want a dog who thinks he's too fancy for the
hunting stuff you want him to do." Don says to Jon.
Don wants the pitbull and Jon wants the Pom.
They do not agree which dog would be best to use.

Don wants a pitbull that is solid and sound. Jon only wants that
Pom. A pit is the kind of dog that can really prowl the ground.
Don shakes his head and says to Jon: "You really need to use
your brain".
So they argue and argue and then argue some more.
They keep arguing to edge of the marsh shore.
And there, lying in wait with a big smile on his face
is the gator with his jaws wide open!

With a loud SNAP! The alligator just misses.
The sound caused the snakes all around to hiss.
The two brothers realize that they are in a whole heap of trouble.
Surrounded by gators and snakes, they finally get out of their
trouble on the double!

We fixing to have a hootenanny like you ain't had in your lifetime.
Hey, this thing is gonna be good." The brothers exclaim.
The visiting Ninja from Asian presents Don & Jon with a great Samurai sword.
The brothers are confused. The Ninja smiles: "Think of it like a sharp 2x4 board."
Now the brothers need to thank this awesome Ninja for the great gift.
They want to do something for him so his spirits can have an uplift.

They immediately take the Ninja Samurai with them on a hunting tour to show
him what real hunting for rednecks means.
There's no other way to bring someone immediate redneck fame!
And so they come across lots of muddy bullfrogs, sneaky legless lizards, snails,
corn snakes, water snakes, tadpoles, and the most dangerous of all the
Mississippi aligator.
The gator attacks the brothers, but the Ninja steps in.
With a few hand gestures, his Ninja magic quickly begins.
The gator goes into a trance and begins to dance.
"This is what is supposed from honest Martial Art men", the Ninja explains.

"This is how a Ninja hunts," the Ninja says.
"Why kill things so they wind up dead?"
"Instead, we let nature present itself in a unique way."
"That is how we can hunt every day!"
So the brothers convince the Ninja to help them hunt poisonous snakes.
That way they don't have to smack their heads with old thatching rakes!
Yet when it is time for the Ninja powers to do their trick,
Jon and Don decide to just hit the first snake they find with a big, big stick.

"That's great, just great," the Ninja mutters, and he disappears into a growing fog.
"Maybe you two brothers just need to go find yourselves a hunting dog."

KWAAAAAAAK!

There's a country club near where John and Don live.
It's a rich place where there's a lot more take than give.
It's also a place where the frogs and snakes are as plump as can be.
It's the best hunting grounds in the world, you see!
So Jon says to Don:
"There ain't nothin' finer than rich snakes' being hunted on a fine golf course."

Jon and Don the twin brother are wearing night-vision goggles, most definitely
trespassing, and doing this for the reward of free frogs and free snakes.

The night-vision goggles also help John and Don see frogs in the dark,
John and Don begin hunting in this rich person's golfing park.
They hunt as long and as fast as they can because they can't wait to smell those
frogs and snakes in their frying pan!

With a good haul in tow, John and Don return home.
That's the place where the snakes and frogs dare not roam!
Yet when they get there, a sound cannot be heard anywhere.
The family looks long and hard everywhere!

Is there a snake hiding out under the house?
Are John and Don being hunted by a big giant mouse?
Is there a herd of rabid beavers ready to take John and Don's hunting score?
John licks his lips... or could there be frogs? Lots and lots more?

But what they find blows John and Don's mind.
It's a Ninja and he sneaks up on them from behind!
"Hello!" the Ninja says. "I'm visiting from Japan."
"I can't wait to smell what you cook up in your frying pan!"

John and Don are redneck twin brothers
to the core.

They love snake hunting - it's their favorite
sport!

They'll go out hunting any time of day or
night.

If there's a snake around, watch out!
John and Don will soon be in sight!

This is a work of fiction. Similarities to real people, places, or events are entirely coincidental.

NINJA COMIC KIDS BOOK FOR AGE 6 - 8

First edition. July 10, 2017.

Copyright © 2017 T. J. Gusman.

ISBN: 978-1386164005

Written by T. J. Gusman.

Dedication

To the most jerky dog in the world that I can luckily call my own and who is inspiring me on a daily basis to come up with these jerky ideas that are helping me inspire other kids from around the world.

Thanks for every moment that I can spend with you and thank you that you are here for me to cheer me up on my darkest days.

Only with your insights and inspiration was I able to turn this project into reality.

All my thanks go to you my dear friend, my partner in crime, and my beloved dog El Ninjo!

Chapter 1: There Ain't Nothin' Finer Than Moonlight Hunting For Snakes n'Frogs

John and Don are redneck twin brothers to the core.

They love snake hunting - it's their favorite sport!

They'll go out hunting any time of day or night.

If there's a snake around, watch out!
John and Don will soon be in sight!

There's a country club near where John and Don live.
It's a rich place where there's a lot more take than give.
It's also a place where the frogs and snakes are as plump as can be.
It's the best hunting grounds in the world, you see!
So Jon says to Don:
"There ain't nothin' finer than rich snakes' being hunted on a fine golf course."

Jon and Don the twin brother are wearing night-vision goggles, most definitely
trespassing, and doing this for the reward of free frogs and free snakes.

The night-vision goggles also help John and Don see frogs in the dark,
John and Don begin hunting in this rich person's golfing park.
They hunt as long and as fast as they can because they can't wait to smell those
frogs and snakes in their frying pan!

With a good haul in tow, John and Don return home.
That's the place where the snakes and frogs dare not roam!
Yet when they get there, a sound cannot be heard anywhere.
The family looks long and hard everywhere!

Is there a snake hiding out under the house?
Are John and Don being hunted by a big giant mouse?
Is there a herd of rabid beavers ready to take John and Don's hunting score?
John licks his lips... or could there be frogs? Lots and lots more?

But what they find blows John and Don's mind.
It's a Ninja and he sneaks up on them from behind!
"Hello!" the Ninja says. "I'm visiting from Japan."
"I can't wait to smell what you cook up in your frying pan!"

KWAAAAAAK!

Chapter 2: Bullfrog Quaking, Snake Hunting And A Mysterious Strange Ninja

We fixing to have a hootenanny like you ain't had in your lifetime.
Hey, this thing is gonna be good." The brothers exclaim.
The visiting Ninja from Asian presents Don & Jon with a great Samurai sword.
The brothers are confused. The Ninja smiles: "Think of it like a sharp 2x4 board."
Now the brothers need to thank this awesome Ninja for the great gift.
They want to do something for him so his spirits can have an uplift.

They immediately take the Ninja Samurai with them on a hunting tour to show
him what real hunting for rednecks means.
There's no other way to bring someone immediate redneck fame!
And so they come across lots of muddy bullfrogs, sneaky legless lizards, snails,
corn snakes, water snakes, tadpoles, and the most dangerous of all the
Mississippi aligator.
The gator attacks the brothers, but the Ninja steps in.
With a few hand gestures, his Ninja magic quickly begins.
The gator goes into a trance and begins to dance.
"This is what is supposed from honest Martial Art men", the Ninja explains.

"This is how a Ninja hunts," the Ninja says.
"Why kill things so they wind up dead?"
"Instead, we let nature present itself in a unique way."
"That is how we can hunt every day!"
So the brothers convince the Ninja to help them hunt poisonous snakes.
That way they don't have to smack their heads with old thatching rakes!
Yet when it is time for the Ninja powers to do their trick,
Jon and Don decide to just hit the first snake they find with a big, big stick.

"That's great, just great," the Ninja mutters, and he disappears into a growing fog.
"Maybe you two brothers just need to go find yourselves a hunting dog."

Chapter 3: The Choice Between A Cute Pomeranian Puppy and a Pitbull Hunter?

Jon & Don, on the other hand, have no clue what just happened
and totally ignore the Samurai's mission.

"You don't want a dog who thinks he's too fancy for the
hunting stuff you want him to do." Don says to Jon.
Don wants the pitbull and Jon wants the Pom.
They do not agree which dog would be best to use.

Don wants a pitbull that is solid and sound. Jon only wants that
Pom. A pit is the kind of dog that can really prowl the ground.
Don shakes his head and says to Jon: "You really need to use
your brain".
So they argue and argue and then argue some more.
They keep arguing to edge of the marsh shore.
And there, lying in wait with a big smile on his face
is the gator with his jaws wide open!

With a loud SNAP! The alligator just misses.
The sound caused the snakes all around to hiss.
The two brothers realize that they are in a whole heap of trouble.
Surrounded by gators and snakes, they finally get out of their
trouble on the double!

But the next day, Jon knows he needs to prove his brother wrong.
He goes and buys that Pom before too long.
Jon is going to show Don that small dogs are the best hunting
dogs. Poms can really crawl into logs to scare out the frogs!

So Jon meets Don that night for another hunting trip.
When Don sees the little dog, the jokes begin to rip.
"What do you call the smallest hunting dog in the word?"
Don asks Jon.
"You call it liquid in a snake's drinking flask!"

"And what kind of hunting can you do with what a small dog can
catch?"
"Why you can play an awesome game of fetch!"
And despite the high hopes that Jon has for his little pom,
that puppy is unable to catch one single frog.

"Real men hunt with real dogs," Don says to Jon.
"Hunting with rats like these is worse than having no fun!"
The Pom begins to run and hide from insulting Don.

Chapter 4: The Hacky Sack

The next day comes as a chance of changing trouble into peace.
It is Hacky Sack day and it would be as fun as fun could be!
To win, one brother has to shoot 10 hacky sacks with a confirmed hit.
The loser would have to clean the winner's hunting kit.

Jon was excited to prove that he was the superior one.
It didn't matter if it had been three years since he'd won.
Today was the day that everything would finally change.
It was time to make become a redneck that was disarranged!

Don, for his part, was ready to make hackey sack art.
He would move faster than a Walmart shopping cart!
The two brothers shared a glare as the time counted down to one.
Then, with a quick whistle, the hackey sack wars had begun!

Jon charges in hard and straight.
Don tries to change up things with a different gait.
Both brothers quickly hit their first hackey sacks quite true,
but then something happens – and neither brother knew
what to do!

You see, snakes converge on them from everywhere.
The brothers try to run, but they can not go anywhere!
"Oh Jon!" Don cries. "I'm sorry I'm better than you!"

Chapter 5: Jokes & Poker

Next the brothers become the town's teacher's worst nightmare because they have another hunch about where the gator might hide.

They hear something in the radio about an aligator that is crawling around in the neighborhood.

Jon & Don want to be good neighbors and they want to save the kids at school from this event.

Later it turns out the aligator thing was just a Southern joke from the radio host.

Both rednecks do not believe the freaky joker and stay alert while playing some poker.

Chapter 6: The Annual Yard Sale

Meanwhile the family holds a yard sale to sell some of their most
valuable possessions like decoys and hunting gear and just everything
they have assembled from around the country.

The twin brothers are still on the lookout for that gator that is
still sneaking around in the woods and they don't exactly appreciate
the fact that their wives and kids go on about this
ridiculous weekend holiday sale.

The aligator is nowhere to be found and that's why the twins are
gearing up for a nasty battle.

Chapter 7: Armored Snakes & Aligator Wisdom

The brothers get their wits back and try to fight.
Turns out the snakes have bulletproof vests, too!
The shots from Jon and Don just bounces away.
The snakes are about to win the day!

As the snakes begin to storm in,
Jon notices in the back stands an alligator with a grin.
"That dadnabit Ninja Gator has come to take our souls!" he cries.
"This isn't the day I want to die."

Then the Ninja Gator yelles out "STOP!"
It becomes so quiet that you could hear someone open a soda pop.
"Let this be a lesson," the Ninja Gator says.
"The next time you hunt in my marsh, you brothers will wind up
dead!"

The Ninja Gator has a whole list of demands.
He puts the list into each brother's hands.
"Let's go over what you can and can't do."
"Let's face it, boys. Ninja Gator don't want to eat you!"

The brothers are told they can hunt no more.

If they want to eat, they have to go to the grocery store.

They can not ever chase a frog around a log again.

If they do, they will become redneck s'mores for all the

Ninja gator's friends.

But it does not stop there – no, it goes on.

You see, the brothers can not even take a gun further than

their lawn.

They have to leave all their hunting equipment at home.

If they do otherwise, they will be eaten where they roam.

"Now boys," Ninja Gator says, "I know this will be hard to

understand."

"But you can still use your guns in the yard."

"Now leave us alone and we'll leave you alone, too!"

"Just realize that your redneck hunting days are through."

John and Don look at each other and look rather sad.

This strange Ninja spell is driving them mad!

But surrounded by armored snakes, there is nothing else they can do.

They agree to the terms.

Their hunting days are through.

Chapter 8: The Redneck Logic Of Don & Jon

You can see John and Don now sitting on a porch every night.

They tell stories about the time the Ninja Gator gave them a fright.

Sometimes when they tell the stories, they look sad and blue.

Curious though...

in their story the brothers ate the gator at a barbecue.

If you head out to the marsh when the day loses its hue,

there's a chance you could meet the Ninja Gator, too.

He's got Ninja wisdom that he's ready to pass right along.

And, if you listen closely, the frogs now sing Ninja souds, too!

About the Publisher

InfinitYou is a hybrid general interest trade publisher. One of the first of its kind InfinitYou publishes physical books, electronic books, and audiobooks in various genres. Our publications are meant to educate, edify and entertain readers of all walks of life from babies to the elderly.

Home to more than twenty imprints such as Infinit Baby, Infinit Kids, Infinit Girl, Infinit Boy, Infinit Coloring, Infinit Swear Words, Infinit Activities, Infinit Productivity, Infinit Cat, Infinit Dog, Infinit Love, Infinit Family, Infinit Survival, Infinit Health, Infinit Beauty, Infinit Spirituality, Infinit Lifestyle, Infinit Wealth, Infinit Romance, and lots more.